CW00865726

This Notebook Belongs To:

....

Printed in Great Britain
by Amazon

32494547R00069